IMAGES
of America

# NEWTON FALLS

This aerial view photograph of Newton Falls shows Falls Steel Tube in between North Center Street and North Canal Street. This photograph also shows the present-day Church of the Nazarene (which was originally St. Mary's Catholic Church/Our Lady of Czestochowa Church) and also shows the east-side cemetery. A train can be seen on the Baltimore & Ohio (B&O) Railroad tracks. (Courtesy of the Newton Falls Public Library, donated by Grace Walmer.)

ON THE COVER: This view is looking east toward downtown Newton Falls on Broad Street. Kloss Hardware, Brown's Market, Neidhart's, and Trumbull Savings & Loan are visible as well as a sign for Route 534. There are many unique vehicles also seen, in addition to a 7-Up truck, which says, "You like it, it likes you," and "Fresh." A traffic light is also present in this photograph, which was taken between 1940 and 1950. (Courtesy of the Newton Falls Public Library, donated by Donna Lou Martin.)

IMAGES
of America

# NEWTON FALLS

Adreanne Foos

ARCADIA
PUBLISHING

Copyright © 2024 by Adreanne Foos
ISBN 978-1-4671-6095-7

Published by Arcadia Publishing
Charleston, South Carolina

Printed in the United States of America

Library of Congress Control Number: 2023947095

For all general information, please contact Arcadia Publishing:
Telephone 843-853-2070
Fax 843-853-0044
E-mail sales@arcadiapublishing.com
For customer service and orders:
Toll-Free 1-888-313-2665

Visit us on the Internet at www.arcadiapublishing.com

*Dedicated to my niece Brooklyn, who had the privilege of growing up in Newton Falls for the first 11 years of her life. Although she is far from home now, I hope she always cherishes the times spent in Newton Falls and, one day, appreciates the history as much as I do.*

# CONTENTS

# ACKNOWLEDGMENTS

I have so many individuals to thank for this book. Foremost, I am so thankful for the Newton Falls Public Library's large collection of pictures, newspaper articles, yearbooks, and artifacts. Elizabeth Carnahan, the local history librarian, deserves special recognition for her invaluable assistance throughout this process. The images in this book were the result of numerous hours of searching and scanning on Elizabeth's part. Unless otherwise noted, all images are courtesy of the Newton Falls Public Library.

I would like to thank my parents, Terry and Brenda Zeleny, who encouraged my love of history. When I was a young child, my dad, who also grew up in Newton Falls, would drive me around Newton Falls in his baby blue 1972 Chevy C-10 pickup truck. While we drove around town, my dad would point out a current business and then proceed to explain to me what the business was when he was growing up. Those trips were what made me fall in love with history, especially local history. Finally, I would like to thank my husband, Jeff Foos. He encouraged and supported me throughout this process of researching and writing, and I am so thankful for his support.

I would like to thank Arcadia Publishing for making my dream of becoming a published author come true. I would especially like to thank Jeff Ruetsch, Caroline (Anderson) Vickerson, and Ryan Vied for their encouragement, guidance, and patience through this whole process. I would like to give a great big thanks to the entire team at Arcadia for the wonderful work they do to make local history accessible to readers around the world.

Last but not least, I would like to thank one of the greatest history teachers I had the privilege of having my sophomore year at Newton Falls High School, Vernon Stamm. Mr. Stamm made learning history fun and really opened my eyes to so many wonderful events in history. He will go down as one the greatest teachers I ever had and a great influence on my love of history.

# INTRODUCTION

The collection of photographs in this book is only a small representation of the history of Newton Falls. There were many more images and newspaper articles I wanted to share, but the collection of images I finally settled on made its way into this book to best represent Newton Falls.

Like many settlements in the northeast Ohio area, the area which is present-day Newton Falls was originally part of the Connecticut Western Reserve. The Connecticut Western Reserve was the name given to the northeast section of Ohio. Eventually, the Connecticut Western Reserve was called Trumbull County. By the early 19th century, Trumbull County was broken up into townships. Newton, eventually named Newton Falls, was part of Trumbull County after the splits and officially became recognized as its own township in 1806. Owners of the township of Newton included Elijah White, Jonathan Brace, Justin Ely, Judson Canfield, Cornelius DuBois, and family. Originally called "Newton" after Newtown, Connecticut, and later called "Newton Falls" after the waterfalls on the Mahoning River, Newton Falls has fluctuated back and forth between a village and a city. Currently, Newton Falls is a village. Despite Newton Falls being a small village, it is filled with so much history.

Newton Falls has always been filled with some sort of industry, which made it popular among workers. Factories, businesses, railroads, canals, mills, and the Ravenna Arsenal made up so much of the industry and provided locals with many jobs. Throughout the 19th century, Newton Falls was also considered a transportation village. The village had access to the early paths made by Indians, to visit the Salt Springs in Weathersfield Township. Then, the Pennsylvania & Ohio Canal made its way through the city, which extended from New Castle, Pennsylvania, to Akron, Ohio, with Newton Falls in the middle. Eventually, the popularity and usefulness of the Pennsylvania & Ohio Canal (nicknamed "the P&O Canal," "the Mahoning Canal," and "the Cross-Cut Canal") dwindled, and the canal land was purchased by railroads. Eventually, CSX, originally known as the Baltimore & Ohio Railroad, purchased the canal land and laid tracks down on the already flat land. The railroad's popularity grew, along with more industry, bringing more and more factories to Newton Falls. Eventually, the Ravenna Ordnance Plant, nicknamed "the Ravenna Arsenal" and now named Camp James A. Garfield Joint Military Training, provided many citizens of Newton Falls with jobs, including two of my relatives, in the 1940s and 1950s.

Due to the East and West Branches of the Mahoning River passing through Newton Falls, bridges were a must. In 1831, a single-lane wooden covered bridge was built over the East Branch of the Mahoning River, connecting Bridge Street to Arlington Boulevard. Eventually, a walkway was added in 1921. In 1856, a double wooden covered bridge, with walkways, was built over the West Branch of the Mahoning River, connecting Broad Street to Charlestown Road and Ridge Road. Although the west bridge was eventually replaced, the east bridge still remains today.

With the growth of industry also came people. With the growing population in Newton Falls, school systems were established as well as many different churches. Many people from all different walks of life lived in Newton Falls, and the many churches and denominations are living proof of a myriad of people coming together in one community, and living together side by side. Together, these folks created Newton Falls. Even within Newton Falls were smaller communities, named Earlville and Arlington Heights, that soon fizzled out at the start of the 20th century but represented individual communities within a village. Earlville, also known as Lower Town, was nestled between both rivers between North Canal Street and North Center Street. Arlington Heights, mostly a housing development, was located along Arlington Boulevard, in addition to Oak Knoll Street, East Broad Street, Superior Street, Woodland Street, Prospect Street, and Maple Drive.

As industry faded in Newton Falls, remnants of the past can still be seen and never forgotten. Although people continue to move away and Newton Falls is now a village, it still holds many people who have never left, who have stayed true to their village and can tell stories about Newton Falls for miles. As many cities have suffered decline and have become known as the Rust Belt, Newton Falls also suffered this tragedy. However, it is important to always remember what came before and where we came from to truly appreciate the village of Newton Falls. Today, the town is known for one of the oldest covered bridges in the state of Ohio, the unique zip code (44444), the waterfalls, and the F5 tornado that hit Newton Falls in 1985, but there is so much more to uncover as you read the chapters that lie ahead.

# One

# THE CONNECTICUT WESTERN RESERVE AND EARLY SETTLEMENTS

The Connecticut Western Reserve, like most early communities in northeast Ohio, was originally inhabited by Native Americans. Various tribes lived in the area that became Newton Falls and the adjacent areas. These early Native Americans built numerous trails, one of which was the Salt Spring Trail. The Salt Springs were originally called Mahonink, which is a Native American term for "salt lick." The name *Mahoning* was derived from the word Mahonink, and thus the Mahoning River was named. The land was reclaimed after the Indian inhabitants died out. The Connecticut Land Company soon acquired this portion of Ohio and renamed it the Connecticut Western Reserve. The area was controlled by the State of Connecticut, and during the late 18th and early 19th centuries, the entire Connecticut Western Reserve was known as Trumbull County. Warren, founded in 1798, served as its capital. The Western Reserve was soon divided into townships, then counties, which still exist today: Trumbull, Portage, Mahoning, Ashtabula, Geauga, and many more. Trumbull County quickly grew to include many new settlements, which included Duck Creek, a little village in the southwest corner of present-day Newton Falls. In addition to Duck Creek, a small village known as Pricetown arose in the south. Soon after these settlements were founded, Newton was established in 1806 and eventually became known as Newton Falls. Roads on the outskirts of Newton Falls are named Duck Creek Road and Pricetown Road, in honor of both original communities.

## Why is it called Western Reserve?

### Part 2

Connecticut's Western Reserve was all considered Trumbull County, with Warren as its capital. On Feb. 10, 1807, Portage County became a separate county from Trumbull. It received its name from the old Indian portage passing through the area.

The entire Western Reserve had been surveyed into townships of 5 miles square by the Connecticut Land Co., under the command of Moses Cleaveland. (5 miles is the size of townships in Connecticut.) The Land Company then sold it to eastern speculators, who in turn sold it to smaller buyers from the east. The Western Reserve was peopled mainly from New England, with pioneers from New York and Pennsylvania adding to the numbers..

This *Villager* newspaper article provides a brief history of the Connecticut Western Reserve, the designation given to the northeast region of present-day Ohio. The article also discusses the Connecticut Land Company, which purchased and sold Connecticut Western Reserve land. Newton Falls was previously part of the Connecticut Western Reserve, which was renamed Trumbull County by 1800, with Warren serving as the county seat. Trumbull County was soon divided into smaller townships. After the Connecticut Land Company survey was completed, Newton was designated as township No. 3, range 5.

This 1800 map depicts the beginning of designating towns within the Connecticut Western Reserve. There was still un-surveyed terrain all the way to the Sandusky Bay area in 1800. The Vermillion River, the Cuyahoga River (spelled Cayahoga on this map), the Rocky River, the Huron River, the Chagrin River (spelled Chagrine on this map), and the Big Beaver River were all present. Newton was founded in 1806 and is not depicted on this map.

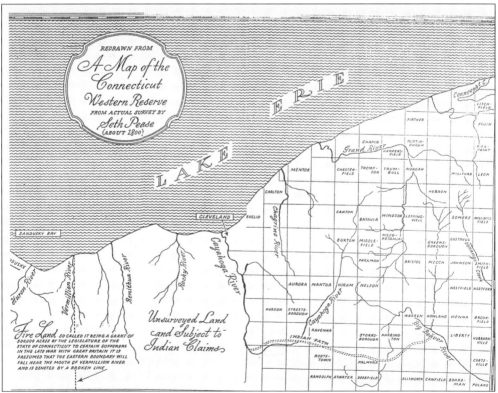

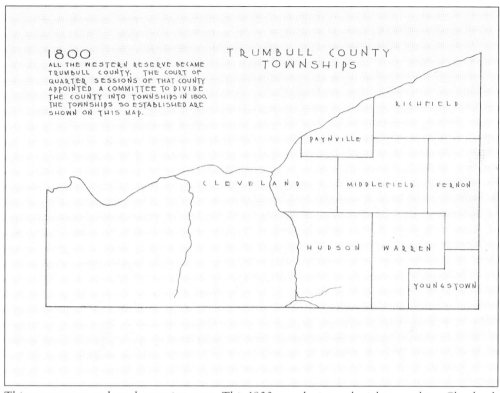

1800
ALL THE WESTERN RESERVE BECAME
TRUMBULL COUNTY. THE COURT OF
QUARTER SESSIONS OF THAT COUNTY
APPOINTED A COMMITTEE TO DIVIDE
THE COUNTY INTO TOWNSHIPS IN 1800.
THE TOWNSHIPS SO ESTABLISHED ARE
SHOWN ON THIS MAP.

TRUMBULL COUNTY
TOWNSHIPS

RICHFIELD

PAYNVILLE

CLEVELAND    MIDDLEFIELD    VERNON

HUDSON    WARREN

YOUNGSTOWN

This map corresponds to the previous map. This 1800 map depicts only eight townships: Cleveland, Paynville (later Painesville), Richfield, Middlefield, Vernon, Hudson, Warren, and Youngstown. This map, like the one before, does not include Newton. These two maps are significant in demonstrating the origins of Newton Falls and the significance of the Connecticut Western Reserve and the Connecticut Land Company for Newton Falls and many nearby communities.

This article was originally published in the *Newton Falls Herald* on March 17, 1988. This article shows the complete counties of the Connecticut Western Reserve, which include Erie, Huron, Lorain, Ashland, Medina, Summit, Cuyahoga, Lake, Geauga, Portage, Ashtabula, Trumbull, and Mahoning. This article also highlights important places and people in the Connecticut Western Reserve, such as the Tallmadge Church, the Ohio Canal, Lanterman's Mill, Battle of Lake Erie, northeast Ohio Indians, and Moses Cleveland's survey in 1796. This map is entitled "The Original Western Reserve."

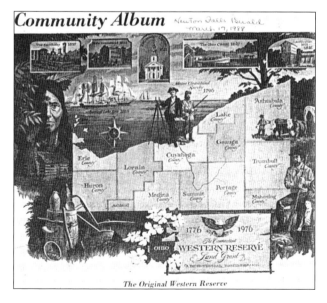

The Original Western Reserve

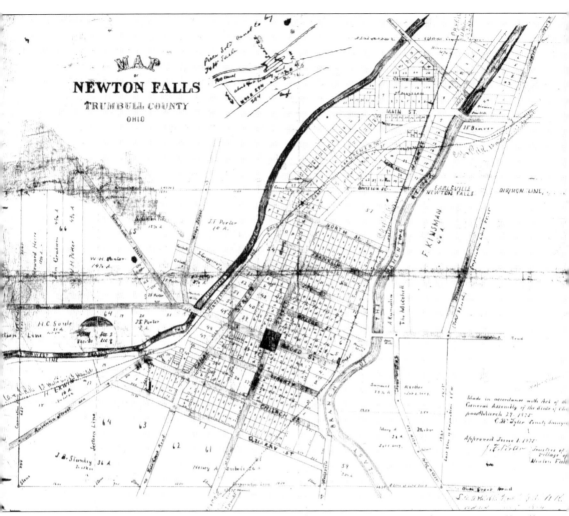

This map is from 1875 and was drawn by C.W. Tyler, a county surveyor. This map was officially approved on June 1, 1875, by the trustees of the village of Newton Falls. This very detailed map shows the abandoned line of the Pennsylvania & Ohio Canal, the East and West Branches of the Mahoning River, streets, and many sections of land and who owned it. Notable names include Harry DuBois and Samuel Kistler. This map also shows Earlville, a small hamlet inside Newton Falls.

# Two

# The Pennsylvania & Ohio Canal and Railroads

Prior to the development of railroads, canals were the main mode of transportation in the United States for both people and commodities. The Pennsylvania & Ohio Canal was built between 1835 and 1840. The 83-mile canal from Akron, Ohio, to New Castle, Pennsylvania, which cost over $1 million to construct (equivalent to $35 million today), passed through a number of locations, including Newton Falls. Newton Falls was important to the P&O Canal for many reasons. Out of the 54 locks needed for the canal, Newton Falls housed one. Lock 22 was located between Lock Street and North Center Street. In addition to Lock 22, Newton Falls also housed one of two aqueducts of the entire canal. The aqueduct, which is a bridge that carries water, typically over a river, was built over the East Branch of the Mahoning River near the current Main Street bridge. In addition to the lock and the aqueduct, the location of both branches of the Mahoning River in Newton Falls made it the ideal place for a canal to follow. During the height of the canal's use, numerous mills were built, as Newton Falls expanded and the ability to import and export products via the canal fueled an industry boom. During the 1860s, canals began to be bought up by railroad companies. The Cleveland & Mahoning Railroad, later the Baltimore & Ohio Railroad and today CSX, bought the land and laid tracks over the canal lands. Today, there are hardly any visible remains of the canal. Lock 22 is buried underneath the ground, the aqueduct ceases to exist, and the towpath is covered. However, one of the last remaining remnants of the canal is Lock Street, named after Lock 22, and it runs close by to where Lock 22 would have stood. After the canals, Newton Falls was home to many sets of railroad tracks owned by several different companies. Today, only the CSX tracks remain in use.

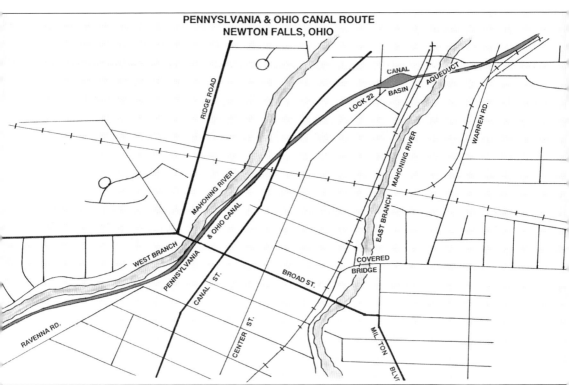

**PENNYSLVANIA & OHIO CANAL ROUTE**
**NEWTON FALLS, OHIO**

This map shows the route of the Pennsylvania & Ohio Canal in Newton Falls. The Pennsylvania & Ohio Canal was known as a feeder canal that was smaller in size than the Ohio & Erie Canal and the Miami & Erie Canal. The canal reached its prime by the 1860s, when railroads became the more efficient way to travel and send goods. The canal land was eventually bought by the Baltimore & Ohio Railroad, where an extension of Baltimore & Ohio tracks was laid north to south. Like the canal, the tracks no longer exist today, but remnants of both can be seen in town.

14

The Baltimore & Ohio Railroad station was located on Franklin Street on top of the hill next to Baltimore & Ohio tracks that ran east and west. The B&O tracks and station were built in 1882. Eventually, Baltimore & Ohio was bought by CSX, and the station was used for CSX employees until March 2011, when a train derailment destroyed the station. This photograph was taken on July 6, 1907.

Baltimore & Ohio had two railroad bridges that crossed the river in Newton Falls. This particular bridge is located over the East Branch of the Mahoning River. Many years after this photograph, Arlington Elementary School was built on the property in front. In the early 1960s, a train derailment occurred on this bridge. Despite the train derailment, the bridge still stands today. This image was taken between 1907 and 1909.

This image of the Baltimore & Ohio Railroad station shows off more of the surrounding area. In this image, a train in the background is heading westbound. Also pictured out front of the station is a horse and buggy. This image also shows the steep hill on the west side. In addition to this hill, another hill was on the east side but is not pictured. A staircase was added on the hill in front of the station where passengers could walk up from Franklin Street. A sign is visible on the side of the station that reads, "Newton Falls."

The Lake Erie, Alliance & Wheeling Railroad (often nicknamed the "LEA&W" and eventually the "Leave Early and Walk") and its station were built in 1876. The station is shown in this photograph from 1895. Before its demise in the 1960s and 1970s, New York Central owned the rail line. Soon the tracks were torn up, and today, a sidewalk has replaced the tracks. For many years, the depot was Bill's Barber Shop and Marge's Beauty Salon, owned by Bill and Marge Kolovich. It still stands today.

On Tuesday, August 7, 1923, Pres. Warren G. Harding's funeral train passed through Newton Falls, traveling westbound on Baltimore & Ohio tracks. The train was on its way to Marion, Ohio, where Harding was to be buried. The train passed through Newton Falls slowly, and many gathered at the site to pay their respects to the late president. This photograph was taken by B.W. Garee.

Another image shows crowds waiting for President Harding's funeral train. Many wait on the tracks in anticipation. Three gentlemen on the left read a newspaper while they wait.

This image depicts children waiting on the tracks for Warren G. Harding's funeral train. A citizen holds a large American flag to pay tribute to the late president.

This image depicts the train coming closer and many of the onlookers watching as it approaches. A man in the foreground is seen pointing at the cameraman. (Courtesy of the Newton Falls Public Library, donated by Barbara Riffel.)

# *Three*

# DOWNTOWN,
# COVERED BRIDGES,
# AND NEIGHBORHOODS

Newton Falls has always had a vibrant downtown, with buildings of all shapes, sizes, and colors. The eclectic mix of buildings makes the downtown area unique. During the 20th century, the downtown housed many familiar businesses, such as Kloss Hardware, Bailey's Furniture, the Manos Theater, Corey Hardware, Neidhart's Insurance, George's Shoe Service & Store, and several bars and restaurants. Today, many of the original buildings still stand and remind those who visit what was once there before. Newton Falls also had two major highways pass through its downtown, Routes 534 and 5. At the corner of East Broad Street and North Canal Street, the two routes crossed. Today, Route 534 still runs through Newton Falls, jogging at the West Broad Street and Ridge Road intersection and also again at the East Broad Street and Milton Boulevard intersection, to continue its north-south run. Route 5 was rerouted in 1969, so it no longer passed through Newton Falls. In addition to a vibrant downtown, Newton Falls once had two wooden covered bridges. Only the east covered bridge remains on the East Branch of the Mahoning River. It was built in 1831, with a walkway added in 1921. The east covered bridge, sometimes referred to as the Arlington Road Covered Bridge, is the second-oldest covered bridge in the state of Ohio. With the bridge being almost 200 years old and after a myriad of repairs, it still proudly spans over the East Branch in its original location. The west covered bridge, built between 1856 and 1860, only spanned the river for 82 years until it was razed in 1942 due to heavy traffic from the Ravenna Arsenal, but it is remembered with fondness among the residents. The west covered bridge was located on West Broad Street near Ridge Road and was a double-lane covered bridge. It also had a walkway for pedestrians.

At the corner of North Canal and West Broad Streets, this image shows many cars stopping at the four-way stop. This was before traffic lights were installed in Newton Falls. A sign for Route 5 is visible on the right-hand side that also points the direction to Akron to the north and Ravenna to the south. Another sign is visible that says Route 534, which runs east to west through Newton Falls. The Butts Mansion is seen on the right-hand side in the background. Union Savings & Trust Bank is seen on the left-hand side. This photograph was taken between 1920 and 1930.

East Broad Street is seen in this image from the early 1910s. In this photograph is the Fair and Corey Hardware store. This image shows cars and a horse and buggy. Several of these buildings still stand today in the downtown section of Newton Falls.

On the corner is Sunoco Oil, a service station for vehicles. Taken in the early 1910s at the corner of West Broad Street and North Canal Street, the First National Bank/the Newton State Bank is seen. The bank eventually changed its name to Union Savings & Trust in 1941.

The post office in Newton Falls is photographed here between 1900 and 1910. The people in this photograph include, starting second from left, Pete Lawrence, postal route 3; Cooke Hudson, postal route 2; children Roy Fenton and Henry Goeppinger; Grace Fenton (dark dress); Julia Keyes (white dress); and Charles Fenton (the postmaster). The photograph was taken by Harry O. Barber. This building once stood on East Broad Street and later became a barbershop.

The double wooden covered bridge, often referred to as "the west covered bridge," was built in 1856 and included a walkway. This bridge spanned the West Branch of the Mahoning River and was a double-covered bridge that allowed traffic from both sides to cross at the same time. In the foreground of this image is a set of tracks, originally belonging to the Baltimore & Ohio Railroad. This bridge was torn down and replaced in 1942 due to the construction of the Ravenna Ordnance Plant. The bridge could not handle the heavy traffic from the Ravenna Ordnance Plant.

This bridge replaced the double wooden covered bridge in 1942. This bridge still stands today and even withstood the F5 tornado in 1985. This photograph was taken between 1942 and 1943, and the Baltimore & Ohio Railroad tracks are visible in this image.

The boat landing is seen here on the west covered bridge. This image was taken looking south, with the walkway on the bridge visible. Water lilies are present in this image and were originally planted by Moody Allen in the 1800s. This image was taken in 1912, and the boat landing, along with several boats and a staircase, is visible. Several mills are seen in the background of this image as well.

The east bridge was built in 1831 and crossed the East Branch of the Mahoning River. This image is from 1908 and shows the bridge before the walkway was added. This bridge still stands today and has undergone many repairs.

A 1940s car can be seen driving westbound in this image, with Broad Street behind the bridge in the background. Looking at this photograph, it shows a wet road, as wet track marks are seen inside the bridge. On the right, a sign is hung on the bridge for Route 534.

The east bridge is shown in this view looking west after the walkway was added on the left side. In this image, a man is visible on the walkway, looking out at the Mahoning River. This bridge and walkway are often associated with an urban legend that is popular in Newton Falls, and the bridge is often called Crybaby Bridge. The urban legend states that a mother and child fell off the side of the walkway and drowned in the mid-19th century. This story was never confirmed and lives on as folklore.

This image from January 1975 shows the east covered bridge in the background and the signpost for Bridge Street and River Street. In addition, the Lake Erie, Alliance & Wheeling Railroad tracks (later New York Central) are shown crossing the road. This image is unique in the fact that there is a myriad of transportation shown—the railroad, the roads, the covered bridge, and the covered bridge walkway.

As Newton Falls grew and expanded, more houses were needed. In the 1920s, Arlington Heights was developed on the east side of the Mahoning River, which included houses between Maple Drive and Arlington Boulevard. Another neighborhood, nestled between both branches of the Mahoning River, was already established as Earlville, nicknamed Lower Town, and was named after Thomas and William Earl, who were early Newton Falls settlers and entrepreneurs. Another neighborhood, founded in the 1940s, was simply nicknamed "the Projects" and was made up of government housing. Although these areas still exist today, the names no longer exist. The area of Arlington Heights was mostly made up of two-story homes, with very similar designs. Later, in 1929, Arlington Elementary School was built to accommodate the growing families and their children. This photograph shows early construction in Arlington Heights at the corner of Broad Street and Warren Road.

The houses in Arlington Heights still stand today. The only indication of this area of Newton Falls once being a small development is the name of the road on which these houses reside. Arlington Boulevard (written as Arlington Road on this photograph) runs east to west and is connected to Bridge Street via the east covered bridge. This view of Arlington Boulevard is looking east toward Warren Road and Bailey Road and shows the houses mid-build.

# Four

# MILLS, DAMS, AND
# THE FLOOD OF 1913

At one time, mills were the main source of production in Newton Falls. Over six different mills existed in town, from grist to paper to wool. These mills produced goods for people to purchase, and goods were also shipped on the canal that ran through Newton Falls. Both branches of the Mahoning River ran through the town, thus both branches saw many mills in the early part of the 19th century. Soon, dams were constructed in the early 20th century on both the East and West Branches of the Mahoning River, and both branches have a set of falls, which is part of the namesake of Newton Falls. Despite the construction of dams on both branches, the Mahoning River still flooded in 1913. The flood of 1913 occurred in the Midwest United States, with rain beginning Easter Sunday, March 23, and lasting through March 26, 1913. The flood was due to rivers overflowing from heavy rainfall, and over 400 people total died in Ohio alone. Because Newton Falls was nestled in between two branches of the Mahoning River, the flooding was unbearable. The flood not only caused overflowing rivers, but also diseases such as typhus and diphtheria. The flood was one of the worst disasters in Ohio history. Despite the terrible flood, both wooden covered bridges survived the treacherous waters. The west covered bridge was even chained to nearby trees by the Butts family to ensure it would not float away. At one point, both branches of the Mahoning River were so flooded that they almost touched and created one giant river.

Eagle Mills, a gristmill, was located on the West Branch of the Mahoning River. Eagle Mills opened in 1829 and was built by Horace and Augustus Stevens. Before Eagle Mills was built, the original gristmill, constructed in 1811, sat in its place but burned in 1817. Also seen in this photograph is the waterfall, which is attributed to the name Newton Falls. On the right-hand side, the home, which now houses Borowski Memorial Home, is seen, in addition to the Butts Mansion on the left.

Eagle Mills and the Porter Mill are seen in this photograph. The Porter Mill was owned and operated by Herman Porter. The Porter Mill, like Eagle Mills, was also a gristmill. (Courtesy of the Newton Falls Public Library, donated by the Byer family.)

This photograph was taken in 1908 of the Hoyle Woolen Mill. This mill was located on the West Branch of the Mahoning River, across from Eagle Mills.

The Kinnaman and Lowry Mill, owned by Jacob Kinnaman and David Lowry, was located on the East Branch of the Mahoning River on First Street. This was the front side of the mill. Although the men in this photograph have not been identified, it is believed that they are workers for the mill. Built in 1852, this mill later became known as "the red mill" and was later moved to North Canal Street. The mill went through different owners, but two particular owners, Thomas and William Earl, owned the mill during the mid-19th century. The brothers also owned property between Center Street and Canal Street. This hamlet was known as Earlville, or "Lower Town," in Newton Falls.

This is the backside of the Kinnaman and Lowry Mill on the East Branch of the Mahoning River. In this photograph, the East Branch waterfalls are on the left-hand side. The buildings sat on a stone foundation on the west side of the river.

This photograph shows a side view of the Kinnaman and Lowry Mill and the front part of the mill.

This panoramic view shows Eagle Mills on the left and the Hoyle Woolen Mill on the right. These mills were built on the West Branch of the Mahoning River.

Known as the Red Mill, this mill stood between North Canal Street and North Center Street after it was moved from the East Branch of the Mahoning River. The mill was sold in the 1970s to clear the land for more business. It was eventually restored and taken to Hale Farm and Village in Bath, Ohio. The mill still stands today at Hale Farm and Village.

Cornelius DuBois owned the property on which this paper mill was built. Soon, DuBois gave the land to his son Dr. Henry DuBois. On this property also sat Dr. DuBois's home, often called "the Mansion" and "the DuBois Mansion." This paper mill burned in September 1907. Several mysteries surrounded the paper mill as to why it had burned. Before it succumbed to fire, the mill was also owned by the Trudely family as a paper mill and then by the Carr family as a flax mill.

This photograph shows the Kinnaman and Lowry Mill on the East Branch of the Mahoning River and the extremely low river. The waterfall is gone in this image. Many people are seen walking around on the river, which has barely any water. This photograph shows the destruction of trees, leading one to believe this was taken after a violent windstorm in 1908.

This photograph shows the woolen mill, but with the waterfall now showing. The East Branch of the Mahoning River is now at its normal level, and the mill is in full use. This photograph was taken between 1825 and 1857.

The hydroelectric power plant dam, shown here in its early stages in 1908, was built on the West Branch of the Mahoning River and replaced the former Eagle Mills and the woolen mill. The base of the hydroelectric power plant is still visible today and serves as a walkway to see the waterfalls.

Another dam excavation took place on the East Branch of the Mahoning River, along with another hydroelectric power plant dam. This hydroelectric power plant replaced the Kinnaman and Lowry Mill on the East Branch. This photograph was taken on July 1, 1908.

The West Branch hydroelectric power plant dam, seen here in 1908, shows workers in the process of building this dam. The rock wall to the right is still visible today and is a beautiful reminder of what was once there on the West Branch of the Mahoning River.

The finished hydroelectric power plant dam is seen on the left-hand side of this image. Taken in 1938, this image also shows the double-covered bridge on West Broad Street. Four years later, the bridge would be replaced.

Taken between March 23 and 26, 1913, this photograph shows the Kinnaman house on the left and the power plant on the right during the flood of 1913. This flood damaged many places in the northeast Ohio area and in other states in the eastern United States.

Taken on First Street between March 23 and 26, 1913, this image shows Newton Steel on the left. A car can be seen driving through the floodwaters. The Mahoning River, which is to the right, was one of the reasons why Newton Falls was flooded so much. A large amount of rainfall caused the river to overflow.

Another view of Newton Steel is captured in this photograph from the flood of 1913. First Street, once known as Mill Street, is seen covered in water, from the overflowed Mahoning River. Nearly 500 people in Ohio died as a result of the flood, and more than 40,000 homes were destroyed in the state of Ohio alone.

Ridge Road is seen here during the flood of 1913. Looking downstream, this photograph shows the overflow of the West Branch of the Mahoning River. The power plant is seen to the right.

# Five

# BUSINESSES AND INDUSTRY

At one time, Newton Falls had many forms of industry, which provided local residents with steady jobs. Factories such as Falls Steel Tube, Rockwell International, the Akron Maderight Tire and Rubber Works, and even the Ravenna Ammunition Plant provided locals with factory jobs, primarily steel mill jobs. The steel boom also encouraged people to start businesses in Newton Falls. Businesses such as Rood's Wallpaper and Paint, Sam's Pizza, James Funeral Home, Borowski Memorial Home, Nussle's Florist, Phillip's Heating Co., Trumbull Pattern Works, and Ed's Barber Shop still exist today, despite the decline of steel factory jobs in the mid-1970s, when most Newton Falls factories closed their doors due to economic recessions. In Youngstown, September 19, 1977, was known as "Black Monday" when one the largest steel mills shut down and more than 5,000 people lost their jobs. Soon, the factories in Newton Falls also shut down, and eventually, Youngstown and the surrounding areas, which included Newton Falls, became known as "the Rustbelt." Despite the current status of being known as the Rustbelt, the steel industry brought many people to Newton Falls for jobs, and many others came to Newton Falls to open their own businesses. Although many jobs and factories have left or closed down in Newton Falls, the list of family businesses still in operation is impressive in such a small town. The saying "Home is where the heart is" holds true for so many locals who have called Newton Falls home for generations.

Rockwell Standard Corporation was founded in 1946 as the Standard Steel Spring Company. The Standard Steel Spring Company utilized the old Newton Steel building on First Street. Following a merger with Timken-Detroit Axle Company, the company became known as Rockwell-Standard Corporation in 1953 and then Rockwell International. On June 11, 1976, the 935 employees of Rockwell lost their jobs due to the plant ceasing operations. The plant made bumpers for Ford, Chrysler, and General Motors vehicles. For a brief time period, Bliss Technologies, a factory similar to Rockwell, was housed in the old Rockwell building until the year 2000. Today, the building is still standing and houses the Newton Falls Recycling Company.

The Newton Steel Co.
Newton Falls
Ohio.

The Newton Steel Company opened in 1923, after four years of building. The company had over 1,200 workers and was so successful, it opened up another plant in Monroe, Michigan. The Great Depression of 1929 caused the Newton Falls plant to close, but the Monroe, Michigan, plant remained open. Many workers from the Newton Falls plant transferred to the Michigan plant. After the Newton Falls plant closed, the Corrigan-McKinney Steel Company opened in the old Newton Steel building in 1934. Finally, it merged with Republic Steel Corporation but closed down again. In 1947, Standard Steel Spring bought the building, and after several more mergers, the company finally settled on the name Rockwell International.

John B. Galletly became plant manager of the bumper division of Rockwell International on July 1, 1970, when this photograph was taken. Galletly transferred from the Ford Motor Company in Owosso, Michigan.

Fred P. Scott was the plant manager of the bumper division from 1936 to 1970. He retired on July 1, 1970, and John B. Galletly took over this position. This photograph was taken on June 24, 1970, one week before his retirement.

The three millionth bumper came off the line at Standard Spring (later Rockwell International) on June 12, 1950. Standard Spring had been in business since July 1947—that is 100 million bumpers per year. Pictured here with the three millionth bumper are, from left to right, William Kirsch, Ray Dillon, Alex McCutcheon, Martin Politsky, and Al Woodford.

On January 31, 1973, Rockwell International made a scholarship donation to Kent State University at Trumbull for $2,500. In this photograph are, from left to right, Douglas Hudson, a Kent State University at Trumbull registrar; William Keyme, the Rockwell plant manager; Pauline Berkowitz, the faculty scholarship chairman; and John Lynn, a Kent State University advisor.

In 1968, Rockwell International welcomed retirees of the company from years past. Twenty-three men and one woman are pictured at the celebration. Many of these retirees would have worked at Rockwell when it was under a different name, specifically Standard Spring Company.

Rockwell International employed 1,000 employees during the time it was open. Pictured here is a worker standing in front of a wall of bumpers. Workers used safety measures like wearing hard hats and safety goggles while on the job. Rockwell International would close its doors officially on June 11, 1976, two days after this photograph was taken.

The Falls Steel Tube & Manufacturing Company opened its doors in the early 1920s and was located between North Canal Street and North Center Street. The owners of Falls Steel Tube were Richard Kenworthy Jr. and Howard Kenworthy. The building was originally Peebles Engineering Company before the Kenworthy Brothers bought the building. Falls Steel Tube produced exhaust pipes, water pipes, and ventilator pipes, and these pipes were sent to various American car manufacturers.

Workers of Falls Steel Tube—Joe Fetcher, Richard Wick, Vick Beltram, and an unidentified truck driver—are seen here in 1950 unloading fuel oil. Workers were constantly moving in this factory to keep up with the demanding job.

Workers at Falls Steel Tube built an addition to the factory. They are seen here with shovels; the foundation is already laid. The growing company was in need of an expansion.

In 1949, two workers are shown in front of a fuel oil tank at Falls Steel Tube. The company was in business for 24 years at this point and produced a majorly successful product for American motor companies.

Falls Steel Tube & Manufacturing Company employed many workers from the Newton Falls area. The factory, which was located between North Canal Street and Center Street, stood in the hamlet of Earlville. Here, workers in the 1950s take a break from work to smile for the camera.

Pictured here are Richard Albert Kenworthy (left) and Howard Kenworthy (right). The Kenworthy family had owned and operated Falls Steel Tube & Manufacturing Co. since its inception in the early 1920s. Richard Kenworthy was the original president of Falls Steel Tube & Manufacturing Co. until his death in 1923. After Richard's death, the company was taken over by a myriad of presidents, including Howard Kenworthy, Fred R. Dresher, Charles Wick Kenworthy, and Victor R. Beltram.

The president of Falls Steel Tube & Manufacturing Co., Richard Albert Kenworthy is photographed here in front of the company during its early days. He is standing in front of a building that says, "Falls Steel." Kenworthy happily got his photograph taken, proud of the legacy he and his family left in Newton Falls through Falls Steel Tube & Manufacturing Co.

Office workers at Falls Steel Tube are pictured here in the 1930s. From left to right are (first row) Doris Lyon and Marjorie Dresher; (second row) Art Bender and Fred Dresher. Although not as physically demanding as the warehouse work at Falls Steel Tube, the office work was just as important to help keep the company and its laborers running smoothly.

John Taylor is shown with a new shaper at Falls Steel Tube in 1948. He is standing around his equipment, which takes up a large amount of space.

Charles Wick Kenworthy, often referred to as "Wick," was photographed in an office at Falls Steel Tube & Manufacturing Co. Kenworthy was acting president from 1962 to 1973. By acting as president of the company, he was following the legacy of his relatives more than 25 years after the company first opened.

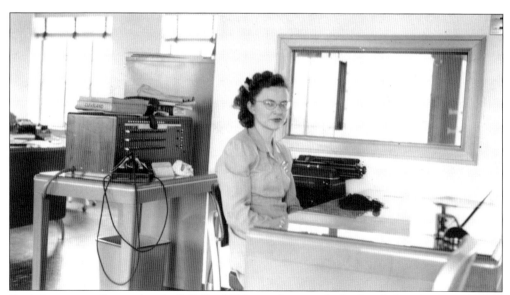

Doris Lyons, an office worker for Falls Steel Tube, is photographed at her desk in 1948. Desk work coincided with the physically demanding work of the factory. Lyons is seen here with a typewriter, an ink pen, and an intercom system.

Falls Steel Tube employees take a lunch break from the demanding conditions of the factory. A room for first aid can be seen as well as the stockroom.

The Akron Maderight Tire and Rubber Works opened in 1920 and had 75 employees but closed its doors in 1922. The structure sat vacant, and in 1936, the Pullman Couch Company from Chicago leased the building and manufactured living room furniture, with 100 employees. After the Newton Falls branch of the Pullman Couch Company dissolved in the 1940s, Luxaire Cushion Company bought the building in 1946, and the company is still in business today. This photograph was taken in 1920 after the Akron Maderight Tire and Rubber Works opened.

Pictured are, from left to right, Russell Riccardi, of Newton Falls Chamber of Commerce; Alan E. Rathburn, the president of Luxaire Cushion Company; Mayor Walter O. Hurd; and Livio DiGiralamo, a local chamber representative. This photograph was taken on February 8, 1962.

Constructed in 1920 on the southwest corner of North Canal Street and West Broad Street, this bank first housed the First National Bank, which moved into this building from a smaller structure that was first established in 1897. In 1922, the name was changed to the Newton State Bank. Finally, in 1924, the name was changed again to the First State Bank. After a sudden closure in 1931, Newton Falls had several branches of banks in the downtown area, but nothing occupied this building until 1937. Union Savings & Trust Bank rented out the building and officially bought it in 1941, where it stayed until the 1980s, when it was bought out by Bank One. This building currently still stands but is empty.

Union Savings & Trust Bank flourished in Newton Falls, especially with its use of technology. Viola Dunlop, photographed on March 15, 1972, is seen here using a television teller screen for customers using the drive-through. Even in the 1970s, this technology was new and advanced.

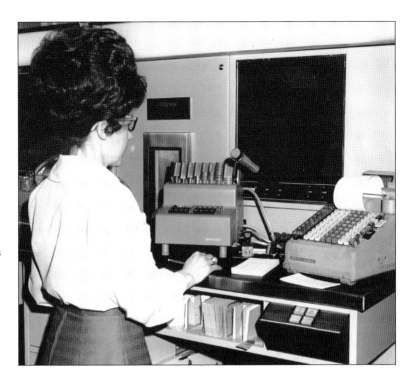

Rood's Wallpaper & Paint, one of the oldest surviving businesses in Newton Falls, was opened in 1947 by Norma and Howard Rood. The Roods ran their business out of their home, in an addition on the side of their house, as pictured. Later, a building was constructed on the front, which remains today. The Roods' legacy was carried on through daughter Wanda and granddaughter Karen and remains in business today.

The Cleveland Cut Flower Company, originally in Cleveland, Ohio, built a branch in Newton Falls in 1913. The first plant manager was W.G. Bate, and the company employed over 30 people. Eventually, the company changed names to the Newton Falls Cut Flower Company and then Nordlie's. Seen in this photograph are, from left to right, Newton Falls mayor Bob Irwin, James Nordlie, Rob Ashton, Fred Ashton (president of Nordlie), and Fred A. Nordlie (the founder of Nordlie's), who is shaking hands with the mayor on September 4, 1980.

The original plant manager, W.G. Bate, is pictured overseeing the construction of the Cleveland Cut Flower Company in 1913. Contractors erecting the Cleveland Cut Flower Company building included F.M. & C.B. Jones, whose name can be seen on the truck behind Bate. The Cleveland Cut Flower Company was located on Center Street, and the building extended south for many blocks.

Originally known as the Strand Theater, the Carol Theater first opened in the early 1920s on North Canal Street, near the railroad bridge and Franklin Street. The theater operated under a Mr. Rubin, from Cleveland, until 1926, when C.S. Tarkowski bought the theater. The theater showed many films until the Great Depression hit, and it closed down for several years. Finally, in 1933, the Raful family bought the theater and renamed it the Carol Theater, after the owner's daughter Carol Raful, who graduated from Newton Falls High School in 1950.

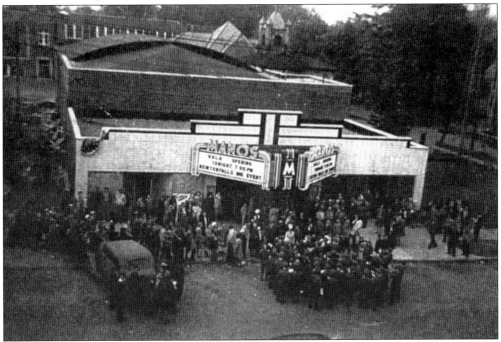

The Manos Theater opened for business on May 22, 1942. The theater was owned by George A. Manos of the Manos Amusement Company. The Manos Amusement Company also took ownership of the Carol Theater in 1941. In this photograph, the old high school building on Center Street is visible as well as the Methodist Episcopal church next to the school and the Christian church (the yellow church) across the street.

Bill Everhart, pictured here, is seen running the projectors for the Manos Theater in May 1948. Projectors 2 and 3 are in this photograph and are branded as Light Master.

The building that housed Carlo's Nightclub and Restaurant has roots back to the early 20th century in Newton Falls. Legend has it that the infamous gangsters Bonnie and Clyde visited this building before it was Carlo's. Carlo's, originally named the Supper Club Cocktail Lounge, was established in 1937. In 1946, the name changed to Carlo's Place and, finally, in 1949 to Carlo's Nightclub and Restaurant. In the 1960s, Carlo's Nightclub and Restaurant was owned by Kenny Ferrance, a local Newton Falls resident who graduated from Newton Falls High School in 1960, and Bill Hyden. In addition to owning Carlo's Nightclub and Restaurant, Ferrance owned and operated the Newton Falls Convenient Store. After the closing of Carlo's, the building eventually housed Mimi's Studio of Dance, owned and operated by Mary Lee Sutton. The building is now home to the New Wave Dance Company.

Carlo's Nightclub and Restaurant was a place to relax, mingle, and enjoy arts and entertainment. Every Friday night from 7:00 p.m. to 10:00 p.m., Irene Johnson played the organ. This photograph was taken in 1973 while Johnson played for the crowd at Carlo's Nightclub and Restaurant.

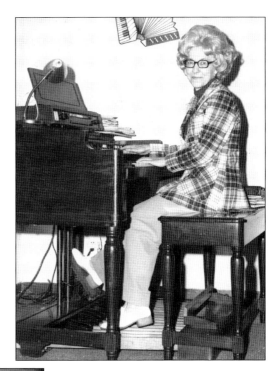

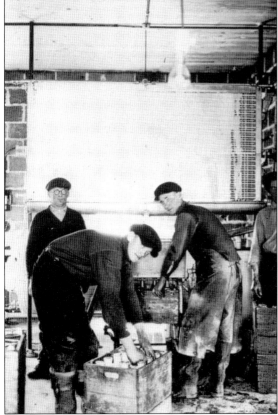

In 1921, Carl W. Burton established the Newton Falls Pure Milk Company, later named Burton Dairy. Burton Dairy was then housed in a small building on the corner of Center and Church Streets. Photographed in 1923 are workers for Burton Dairy, including Carl Burton, Louis Perry, and Emmett Finnical.

The Burton family's patriarch, Carl Burton, is photographed with his family in 1927. Pictured with Carl is his wife, Marjorie Burton (left), and daughters Helen Burton (standing) and Marjorie Burton (sitting).

The building in which Burton Dairy operated out of was located on Center Street. This photograph was taken in 1928 and shows off a thriving dairy business for the Burton family.

Burton Dairy deliveryman Jesse Bailey is photographed delivering milk in 1942. The horse, named Old Bill, pulled the milk truck for Bailey. Behind the milk truck and Old Bill is a home that is still standing today and serves as the Newton Falls Area Chamber of Commerce building.

Another photograph of Burton Dairy shows the side of the building. In the front part of the building, Burton Dairy sold ice cream. In addition to ice cream, the company produced milk, cottage cheese, buttermilk, and cream.

Burton Dairy came to fruition in 1921. This was the original building for Burton Dairy before the company to the corner of Center Street and Church Street. The family resided in a house on Church Street, near the dairy, for easy access to the business.

Marge & Bill's
Beauty
and
Barber Shop

Bill's Barber Shop and Marge's Beauty Salon occupied the former Lake Erie, Alliance & Wheeling Railroad station. The barbershop first opened in 1968, and in 1969, Marge opened up a beauty salon. After the barbershop closed, a bakery opened in its place, still preserving the railroad station. Pictured on the left is Bill the barber with his grandson Jake Byers, Marge and Bill Kolovich are on the top right, and the railroad station in which the barbershop and beauty shop resided is on the bottom.

The *Newton Falls Herald* was originally known as the *Newton Falls Review*, the *Newton Falls Independent*, and the *Tri County News*, established as early as 1875. The original building, seen here, was located on South Canal Street on the southeast corner. Pictured here are the editor John Green and Cora Bonner, a linotype operator who was employed for the newspaper from 1898 to 1941. This photograph was taken in the early 1900s.

William E. Hacker (left) and Arthur Bender (right) are pictured reading a *Newton Falls Herald* newspaper from July 1966. The paper highlights the festivities in Newton Falls from Independence Day. Hacker was the editor and publisher of the *Newton Falls Herald* from 1937 to 1944. He was living in California at the time of this photograph but was staying with Arthur Bender while visiting the *Herald*.

Phillip's Heating Co. was established in Newton Falls in 1938. This clipping from the *Newton Falls Herald* celebrates the 50th anniversary of the business. Phillip's was co-owned by Jack Sutton and Phil Elliott during the 50th anniversary, and the business still serves Newton Falls today. It is one of the oldest businesses left in town, in addition to Rood's Wallpaper, Sam's Pizza Shop, Borowski Memorial Home, and James Funeral Home. Phillip's Heating Co. focuses mostly on installing and repairing air-conditioning and heat systems.

NEWTON FALLS HERALD—Wed., March 7, 1984—13

Phillips Heating

The staff of Phillips Heating serves you fast and efficiently.

## 50th Anniversary

Jack Sutton and Phil Elliott share both the joys and the responsibilities as co-owners of Phillips Heating Company located on S. Canal St., Newton Falls.

The company is now celebrating 50 years of sales and service to Newton Falls, Windham, Southington, Leavittsburg, Wayland, Lake Milton and other communities in the surrounding area.

Sutton has been an active partner in Phillips Heating 27 years. Elliott, the more recent member of the partnership, was appointed by the Trumbull County Commissioners to serve on the Trumbull County Heating Board, a branch of the county's building inspection department.

Phillips Heating employs ten persons offering services which include the installation of gas, oil and electric heating systems, air conditions, heat pumps, wood and coal stoves, water heaters and all types of energy saving equipment for residential and commercial needs.

Trumbull Pattern Works moved from Leavittsburg to Newton Falls in 1965 and was owned and operated by Clayton Reakes II. The company was eventually passed down to Clayton Reakes III, who still owns this business today. The building in which Trumbull Pattern Works moved to in the 1960s was originally the Andrews Bowling Alley. The company utilizes wood patterns to create parts for the steel industry in the United States and Canada. This photograph was taken at Trumbull Pattern Works on February 26, 1986.

The post office pictured here was housed in the Masonic Temple temporarily, while it moved several times on West Broad Street. At one time, the post office was housed in the Corey Hardware building. Pictured are, from left to right, C.R. Finnical, the postmaster; Oscar Woodward; and Florence Finnical, a clerk for the post office. Finally, after several moves, the post office moved to a building located at 28 North Canal Street in 1953, where a McDonald's presently stands. After the F5 tornado, the post office moved to Ridge Road into an older roller rink, where it still stands today.

*Six*

# THE COMMUNITY CENTER AND THE RAVENNA ARSENAL

The Ravenna Ordnance Plant, sometimes referred to as the Ravenna Ammunition Plant and the Ravenna Arsenal, was built between 1940 and 1942. The arsenal is close to 22,000 acres and spans over Trumbull and Portage Counties. Before the construction of the arsenal, more than 250 families were asked to leave their homes, as the government acquired the land to build the arsenal. The families were given 30 days to move and were also paid to leave their homes. In addition to the homes, a Boy Scout camp, Camp Skudcwecook, was also on the property that the government purchased. The government paid the Boy Scouts of America $53,000 for their 200-acre camp. After the arsenal was constructed, the facility built bombs and housed ammunition at the start of World War II; it also operated during the Korean War and the Vietnam War. The 22,000-acre piece of land is fenced off and is not open to visitors. Today, the arsenal is named Camp James A. Garfield Joint Military Training Center and is still as secretive as ever. Because the arsenal was built so close to Newton Falls, a United Services Organization (USO) Club was also constructed in 1941 on Quarry Street for soldiers and their families. After World War II, the arsenal sold the building to Newton Falls, and it reopened as the Community Center. Because the arsenal was built so close to Newton Falls, it caused the town to expand its residents and businesses, thus causing Newton Falls to become a popular spot during the time of the arsenal.

Built in 1941 and dedicated in 1942, the Community Center was originally known as the United Services Organization, or the USO. The building originally served as a recreational facility for the workers of the Ravenna Ordnance Plant and their families. The building was only used in this capacity until 1945. The USO Club was sold by the Ravenna Ordnance Plant to Newton Falls in 1947 for $10,000. The Community Center still stands today but was recently deemed unsafe to use by the City of Newton Falls.

The Community Center served the community in various ways after it was sold by the Ravenna Ordnance Plant. Dances, weddings, school activities, and so much more occurred in this building. This postcard, printed between 1948 and 1953, depicts the building surrounded by beautiful trees. The Community Center sits on 10 acres of property, which are used today for the city park.

A group of ladies, believed to be wives of Army men, gathered around the fireplace at the USO Club on February 6, 1942. A USO flag is seen on the left-hand side. The ladies are seen mingling, reading newspapers, and enjoying each other's company, all while dressed to the nines.

Citizens of Newton Falls gather with war officials in 1942 at the USO Club. During this time, World War II was looming heavily over everyone in the nation, especially in Newton Falls. The USO Club was a constant reminder of the war because the club was built by the Ravenna Ordnance Plant for families of servicemen.

Although the men were off to war, the women of the USO Club made it a priority to socialize. This photograph was taken in 1943 and shows, from left to right, Mildred Kopko, Jean (Young) Powell, June (Wallace) LaCoque, Ann (Finnical) Grim, Sarah (Stanley) Stutz, Sarah Jones, Jean Tavalaro, Margaret "Peg" (Vasco) Berrigan, a Mrs. Rice (Christian Church minister's wife), and Helen (Sloban) Gillette.

The opening ceremony of the USO Club occurred on February 6, 1942. This photograph depicts a group enjoying the new club building. Not everyone in this photograph is identified, but at left is Art Bender. Irma Hurd is seen here with the USO badge proudly displayed on her right arm. Bertha Daniel, the director of the USO, is sitting next to Irma Hurd.

During the dedication service for the USO Club in 1942, Mayor Wallace Elmo Bailey gave a speech dedicating the club to the servicemen. Mayor Bailey was active in choosing the location where the USO Club would be built. He is quoted by the *Newton Falls Herald* as saying, "We here in Newton Falls want to fulfill our duties in this great defense effort so as to bring credit to ourselves, our community and our own United States." This quote, along with the article in its entirety, was featured on the front page of the *Newton Falls Herald* on January 23, 1942.

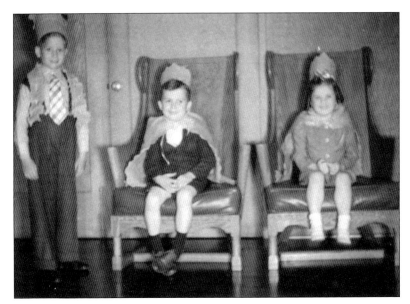

Many events took place not only for the wives of servicemen, but also for their children too. In 1942, a king and queen were selected among the youth. The king was Gary Linscott, and the queen was Karen Landis.

Inside the USO Club building were several small rooms, a shared community space with a fireplace, and an auditorium with a stage. This room was dedicated as a playroom, or clubroom, for the children of servicemen. Children can be seen playing checkers and reading on the floor of the clubroom.

Members of the Kiwanis Club are seen here entertaining at the USO Club. The sign says, "Wise-Man Sewall / Zee-Pump-O." On the left is George Sewall, and on the right is White Ogan Jr. This photograph was taken between 1942 and 1943.

The USO Club featured many events. This photograph shows the Ruth Auteneiths Orchestra on stage performing for the members of the USO Club. The orchestra is small but mighty, with a drummer, a saxophone player, and a piano player.

On June 1, 1942, the Hunkin-Conkey Construction Company began construction on the Ammonium Nitrate Plant at the Ravenna Ordnance Plant. Although the Ravenna Arsenal spans over many counties, it has direct ties with Newton Falls due to the USO Club building. The plant provided many citizens of Newton Falls with jobs. This is an official photograph of the Ravenna Ordnance Plant.

This photograph was taken at approximately 12:00 p.m. on December 30, 1941. The aerial view shows many buildings, including WS-2A, WS-1A, WS-1, WS-3A, and WS-3. This photograph was taken from the intersection of Newton Falls Road and George Road.

Looking west, the final touches for the Ammonium Nitrate Plant are shown. The image was taken in 1942, and soon, this building would see a lot of action for the World War II effort.

Railroad tracks were essential to the Ravenna Ordnance Plant. Baltimore & Ohio tracks split from the main line off Route 5 and entered the arsenal on two lines. Only the railroad bridges were ever visible from Route 5 going into the plant. This image, taken on September 20, 1942, shows the Ammonium Nitrate Plate finished, with the tracks being laid out front.

Needing its own water tower, which can be seen in the background, the Ammonium Nitrate Plant is seen in this 1942 photograph. It was finished and used at this point in the war. Many employees from Newton Falls held steady work at this plant.

The railroad tracks that went into the arsenal were important, especially for importing and exporting materials. This photograph, taken in 1942, shows the railroad tracks going into the powerhouse being laid by several workers from the Hunkin-Conkey Construction Company.

Taken on December 26, 1941, at approximately 3:00 p.m., this image shows the repair shop from the ground view. A man is seen walking through the mud, and several cars are parked in front of the repair shop. This was taken the day after Christmas and 19 days after the attack on Pearl Harbor, which only upped the war efforts even more at the Ravenna Ordnance Plant.

The laboratory, firehouse, laundry station, motor repair, powerhouse, and maintenance building made up part of the little village of the Ravenna Ordnance Plant. This photograph was taken after a snowfall on December 30, 1941, at approximately 11:55 a.m. George Road is the main thoroughfare in this image.

Although the Ravenna Ordnance Plant is still a mystery even after 80 years, glimpses into the arsenal are rather intriguing. Seen here are the cafeteria, print shop, and hospital that created another little village inside the plant. This photograph, like the last, was taken on December 30, 1941, at approximately 11:55 a.m.

# Seven

# PUBLIC SCHOOLS, CHURCHES, AND GOVERNMENT BUILDINGS

As Newton Falls expanded with people, a need for government buildings, churches, and schools arose. Government structures included a town hall, a fire station, and a municipal building. The public school systems in Newton Falls can be traced back to as early as 1812. There were several one-room schoolhouses in Newton Falls until 1857, when a school building was erected on Center Street. Another building was constructed in the same spot in the 1860s, with a bell tower. After 80 years of use, a new high school was built yet again in the same spot, and it included a junior high wing and an elementary wing, called Central Elementary. That school was in use for close to 80 years as well when the F5 tornado destroyed part of it. Another and final high school was built on Milton Boulevard in 1985. In addition to the high school building, the property on Milton Boulevard also housed the middle school, constructed in 1971. An elementary school was built in 1929 called Arlington Elementary. Arlington Elementary was on Arlington Boulevard in a small hamlet of Newton Falls called Arlington Heights. The school was in use until 2008, when it was demolished and another elementary school was built on the same property as the middle school and high school. The middle school became the elementary, while the new school building became the middle school. Presently, Newton Falls Elementary School students have been moved into the middle school building due to the declining population. The former elementary school, which was the former middle school, is now a day care. When people moved into this area, many types of religions also followed. Newton Falls had many denominations of churches from its inception: Catholic, Methodist, Lutheran, Episcopal, Nazarene, and so on. When an eclectic group of people show up in one area, there are bound to be differences, which then leads to more church buildings. Today, Newton Falls still has many churches, and many are rooted back to when the town was established.

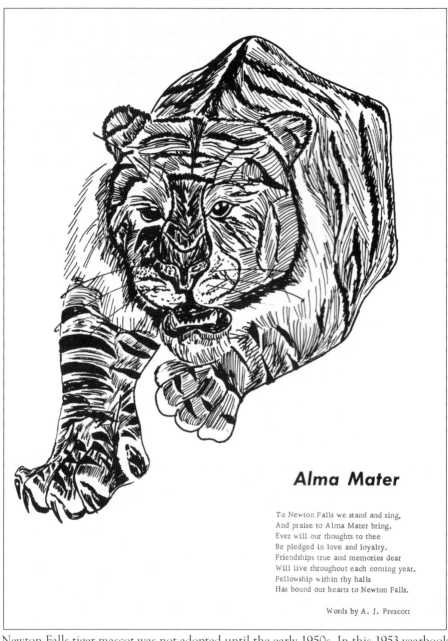

## Alma Mater

To Newton Falls we stand and sing,
And praise to Alma Mater bring.
Ever will our thoughts to thee
Be pledged in love and loyalty.
Friendships true and memories dear
Will live throughout each coming year.
Fellowship within thy halls
Has bound our hearts to Newton Falls.

Words by A. J. Prescott

The Newton Falls tiger mascot was not adopted until the early 1950s. In this 1953 yearbook, the Newton Falls High School alma mater, written by A.J Prescott, reads, "To Newton Falls we stand and sing, and praise to Alma Mater bring. Ever will our thoughts to thee, be pledged in love and loyalty. Friendships true and memories dear, will live throughout each coming year. Fellowship within thy halls has bound our hearts to Newton Falls." The alma mater was sung to the tune of the hymn "Come, Christians Join to Sing." The melody of this hymn came from Madrid, while the lyrics for the hymn were written by Christian H. Bateman. The name of the yearbook, *NEFAO* (for Newton Falls, Ohio), was adopted in 1953. From 1950 to 1952, the yearbook was called *The Mirror*. From 1945 and 1949, the yearbook was called *The Tiger* (but no mascots were present during this time). Finally, from 1940 to 1944, the yearbook was called the *New Fallian*.

In 1812, Newton Falls had several small school buildings. One school in particular was on a farm, which was a far distance for many of the students. In 1857, another schoolhouse was constructed in the center of town but was replaced soon after in the 1860s by a larger, brick building, which is seen here on Center Street. The first commencement took place in 1878, with two graduates, Sadie Bosworth and Fannie Filley. This building stood until another brick school was erected in 1922 to house the growing population.

Newton Falls High School, built in 1922, was used until 1985 when an F5 tornado destroyed the junior high section. The school went through several changes and additions in the 1950s. In addition to Newton Falls High, Center Street Elementary School was also on the property, next to the high school. A corridor was added in 1951 to connect the two buildings. In addition to the corridor, a public library, several more classrooms, and a junior high school wing were added. The high school building still stands today on Center Street and is owned by the Cadle Company.

# "THE OLD SCHOOL"

---

## Alumni of the Newton Falls High School, who will be Asked to Help the Library.

---

In view of the movement to interest the alumni of Newton Falls schools in the enlargement of the school library, we print below a complete list of the High School alumni. Doubtless a perusal of the names will be found interesting to many as serving to revive memories of the associations of school days here. The list totals 274, of whom 17 are deceased:

Class of '78—Fannie E. Filley, Sadie B. Bosworth.

Class of '79—Harvey A. Fiester, Cora Nina I. Barber, Chloe A. Tate, Carrie M. Hoover, Ella E. Kane.

Class of '97—Oscar Smith, Alice M. Pleuss, Frank J. Bussey, Flora W. Klingensmith, William Thomas, Goldie M. Hipple, Alice M. Butts, David J. Bricker, Catherine P. Wilson, Arthur E. McClure, Anna E. Moon, Henry C. Church, Jr., Leroy W. McCreday, Lillie M. Meeker, John T. McKibben, Frances H. Leyde.

Class of '98—George F. Flory, Wade K. Gardner.

Class of '99—Carrie E Klingensmith, Minnie M. Goeppinger, Sarah K. Pierce, Chloe E. Yeager, Lillian E. Butts, Blanche M. Everett, Charles F. Becker, Lewis W. Williams.

Class of 1900—Esther I. Bricker, Mabelle E. Long, Erma H. Hoover, Ethel B. Johnson, Grace G. Smith, Gertrude E. Flick, Charles H. Gillett, Florence A. Becker, Clyde C. Pierce, Floyd S. Williams.

Class of '01—Edwin Little, Mamie

This article was published between 1915 and 1922. It lists the alumni of Newton Falls High School dating back to 1878. The article was to pay tribute to those who graduated from Newton Falls High School during its first 40-plus years.

The high school building was also connected to the junior high on the right-hand side. During the 1985 tornado, the junior high was destroyed as well as the gymnasium. The library and high school still stand today, but the junior high school is now an empty parking lot.

Newton Falls Middle School was built in 1971 on Milton Boulevard. Originally, this school was meant to be the new high school, but after several failed attempts to push that idea, it stayed a middle school. A new middle school building was constructed in 2004. In 2009, the middle school became the elementary school, and Arlington Elementary School was torn down.

Arlington Elementary School is pictured here in 1931. This was before the two additions were added on both sides. Arlington Elementary School was named after a hamlet within Newton Falls called Arlington Heights. Arlington Heights extended down Arlington Road and went as far south as Superior Street. Many of the homes there were first built in the 1910s and 1920s, with the addition of the elementary school in 1929 for the growing population. Children are seen playing on the playground, and some children are riding their bicycles.

On September 1, 1965, Arlington Elementary School extended the school's playground by adding blacktop to the area. Workers are seen spreading the blacktop around. The additions to the school had already occurred, and more room for a playground was much needed for the growing school.

Construction began on Arlington Elementary School in 1928. The school building was located on Arlington Street and sat to the east of the single-lane covered bridge. Sewer construction is seen in this photograph, along with three workers. Arlington Elementary School was situated in Arlington Heights, a hamlet within Newton Falls, similar to Earlville. Additions to Arlington Elementary were constructed in the 1950s and consisted of two new wings of classrooms on both sides of the building. Arlington Elementary was used until 2008, when it was demolished. A surviving brick is on display at the Newton Falls Public Library local history room.

A senior class photograph from 1935 shows a total of 67 students in the graduating class. In addition to the graduating students, D.L. Buchanan, the school superintendent, and Thos O. Griffiths, the principal, are pictured. Elton Ewing was the class treasurer, a Miss Conklin was the class advisor, Frank Pitcovich was the class president, and Bruce Swart was vice president. Many of the students' families stayed in Newton Falls for years after this.

The 1942 football team, consisting of 33 players and three coaches, ended the football season on a high note. The team played a total of eight games and won six out of those eight games. This image does not show the tiger mascot, which was not adopted until the early 1950s. The players are wearing dark and light jerseys, which could denote varsity and junior varsity players.

In 1953, Newton Falls High School cheerleaders raised money for uniforms by selling mums and tiger pins. This was the first group of cheerleaders at Newton Falls to raise money to buy uniforms. Cheerleaders before 1953 did not have uniforms. This was also one of the first sightings of the tiger mascot.

The 1927–1928 school year at Newton Falls High School consisted of 11 faculty members. The faculty are seen standing on the front staircase of the Newton Falls High School Building. From left to right, the faculty members are identified as (first row) Mesdames Adams, Beavers, Ewing, Webb, Jenkins, and Phillips; (second row) Messrs. Heasley, Leiter, Glass, L. Leiter, and Griffith.

**FACULTY OF THE NEWTON FALLS HIGH SCHOOL 1927--1928**

First Row, left to right—Mesdames Adams, Beavera, Ewing, Webb, Jenkins, Phillips.
Back row, left to right—Messrs. Heasley, Leiter, Glass, L. Leiter, Griffith.

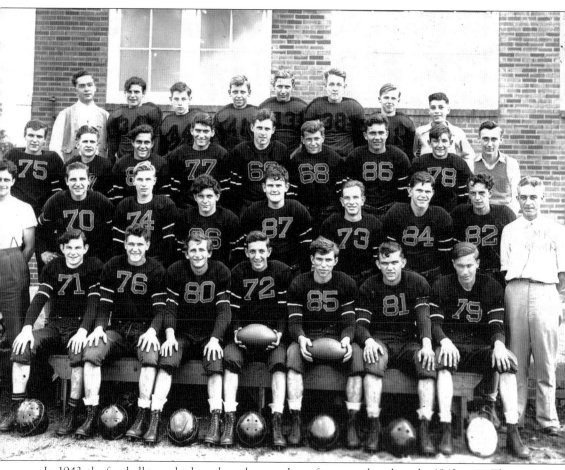

In 1943, the football team had one less player and two fewer coaches than the 1942 team. The tiger mascot is still not visible, nor is the name of the high school on the jerseys. Several of the students from the 1942 football photograph are seen with the same number on their jerseys.

St. Joseph's Roman Catholic Church, pictured in a snowstorm in the 1940s, was built in 1923. It stood on the corner of Quarry Street and Ravenna Road. Rev. Francis P. Tomanek was appointed the first priest at St. Joseph's Roman Catholic Church. This structure no longer stands today, but a new church building was erected to the right and is still standing.

The Methodist Episcopal Church in Newton Falls was organized in 1836. Pictured here is a Sunday school class in the 1930s. The church building pictured was constructed beginning in the early 1900s, but previously, the members of the Methodist Church met in Lower Town in a small school building until their first structure was erected near the present-day railroad underpass on Center Street. Baltimore & Ohio, now CSX, later bought the first church building and land for $7,000. The new church building pictured above was dedicated on February 12, 1905. An organ for the church was purchased in 1927. This building no longer stands today and was demolished in 1958, but a new Methodist church stands on Ridge Road.

The Evangelical Lutheran Church has its roots as far back as 1837. In the latter half of the century, two Lutheran groups used the first church building (later the Newton Falls Town Hall on Bailey Road), located on present-day Newton Tomlinson Road, for services. The German Reformed Lutherans used the building for their services on Sunday mornings, while the German Lutherans used the structure for their services on Sunday afternoons. Soon, the two communities merged and formed the German Lutheran Church, later changed to the First English Lutheran Church. Finally, it was named the Evangelical Lutheran Church, and a new building, pictured, was constructed in 1910 and still stands today. In 1940, the Lutheran community faded in Newton Falls, and the building was sold to the Greek Catholics. Today, the church is still in operation as FWD Church, a nondenominational church.

Taken between 1927 and 1930, this interior photograph of the Methodist Episcopal Church, located on Center Street, shows off elegant designs. The rounded pews are unique to the building. An upright bass and an organ are seen in the background. The building was dedicated in 1905 and used until 1958.

This exterior photograph of the Methodist Episcopal Church shows the bell and stained glass windows. To the right of the church, Newton Falls High School is present. On May 10, 1939, the church's name was shortened to the Methodist Church and "Episcopal" was dropped. Nineteen years later, the church would be demolished, and the vacant lot would be used for the Newton Falls High School.

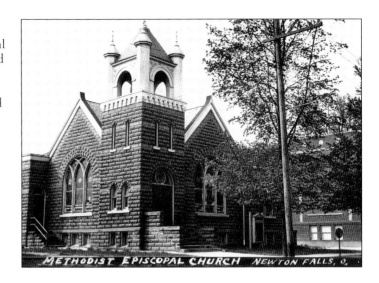

The sanctuary for the Methodist Church was built in 1964, and ground was broken on Easter Sunday. The first service was held on March 28, 1965. From 1958 to 1965, the church met at the present location, which only consisted of a fellowship hall and several classrooms. The sanctuary was constructed next to these wings of the church. The church saved the Good Shepherd window from the original Methodist Episcopal Church on Center Street, and it was placed in the current structure's prayer room as a reminder of the members who came before.

The Old Disciple Church, also known as the Disciples of Christ, was built between 1838 and 1839. The church was located on North Canal Street, near the Baltimore & Ohio Railroad bridge and the Pennsylvania & Ohio Canal. Pictured is the entire congregation by the front entrance. This photograph was taken in 1877.

The First Congregational Church, pictured here in 1910, was located on the corner of North Center and Jay Streets. The roots of this church can be traced back to 1840, but a building was not dedicated until March 16, 1842. It was used until May 17, 1959, when a new church building was constructed at the corner of Charlestown Road and Fifth Street. In 1962, the congregation became part of the United Church of Christ but retained its original name, the First Congregational Church. The church remained open until 2020, when the village of Newton Falls purchased it to use for its administrative building.

St. Michael's Greek Catholic Church was established on August 6, 1922. Originally located on Arlington Road, the church moved locations into the former Lutheran church on Quarry Street. Soon, that building was outgrown, and a bigger facility was needed. Groundbreaking began on October 13, 1968, on Ridge Road. Fourteen months later, the new church, pictured here, was completed, and the first service held in St. Michael's was Christmas Eve in 1969. St. Michael's purchased land in 1922 on Newton Tomlinson Road for their cemetery, which is still used today. The Lutheran, or German, cemetery is directly next to St. Michael's Greek Catholic Cemetery.

The Messiah Lutheran Church dates back to July 5, 1955. Although the congregation did not have a church to worship in, Rev. John E. Berger utilized the Community Center, the former USO Club, for worship gatherings for the Messiah Lutheran Church. In 1958, the congregation bought the former Congregational church building on the corner of Jay and Center Streets. The first service that was held in that building for the Lutherans was on Pentecost on May 17, 1959. After using the former Congregational church for three years, it was decided that the church would erect its own building. Finally, in 1966, the new Messiah Lutheran Church was built on the northeast corner of Fairport and Ridge Roads, and it still stands today.

St. Mary's Roman Catholic Church was established in 1928 as Our Lady of Czestochowa Church, with Polish roots. It occupied what is now the Nazarene Church on North Canal Street. In the 1940s, while World War II was raging, a complex of buildings was erected on the corner of Maple Drive and Milton Boulevard to accommodate the women and children of servicemen in World War II. The US government constructed this building. Soon, it was purchased by Bishop A. McFadden and he planned to turn part of the complex into a Catholic school. He succeeded in doing so. The building was eventually demolished, and a new structure, St. Mary's Social Hall, was erected. The new structure eventually turned into St. Mary's Catholic Church, and the former church was sold. On May 13, 2008, St. Joseph's Roman Catholic Church and St. Mary's Roman Catholic Church consolidated into one church, becoming St. Mary and St. Joseph Church.

The First Christian Church, originally a Baptist church, was incorporated in 1820. In 1839, a church was built on North Canal Street, near the present-day library. The church worshiped here for almost 70 years. In 1908, the Baptist church, or "the Yellow Church," was built on North Center Street and still stands today. In 1925, the Baptist congregation dissolved and became the First Christian Church. Pictured is the First Christian Church in the 1970s during a snowstorm.

The city hall and fire station were housed in this building from 1891 to 1949 on North Canal Street. This building also had a small jail cell. This structure was torn down in 1949 and replaced with the current municipal building, which still houses the jail and fire station.

On October 17, 1862, the Masonic Lodge was established in Newton Falls. It was named Newton Falls Lodge No. 462. Fifteen masons originally established this lodge in Newton Falls. This photograph, taken in 1925, shows off the Masonic Lodge building on the southwest corner of South Center Street and West Broad Street. The building is still in use as a Masonic Lodge today.

This Newton Township Hall photograph was taken by Robert Irwin between the years of 1905 and 1910. This structure was originally a Lutheran church, located on Newton Tomlinson Road, and was later moved to Newton-Bailey Road and became the town hall building until 1978. Currently, a new town hall building stands in this location, which was constructed after the original town hall structure was demolished.

A new sign for the Newton Township Offices, which included the trustees, the police department, and the road department, was placed on the site of the town hall on Newton-Bailey Road in June 1986. The newly built town hall, to the left but not shown, was constructed in 1978 and was only eight years old when the new sign was put up.

ty Hall,
ewton Falls O.

This image shows a side angle of city hall. Like the image on page 93, it shows the fire station. It was noted that this building had a steep staircase up to the second-floor offices. Next to this building was the office of Dr. E.G. Kyle.

The current-day municipal building, located on North Canal Street, was built in 1949. This image was taken in 1961, and to the left is a house that is no longer standing. The building houses the fire station and jailhouse.

# Eight

# Notable People, Events, and Houses

Newton Falls had many well-known residents and homes during the 19th and 20th centuries. David Tod, the 25th governor of Ohio, resided on Liberty Street in the Tod Home for several years. Along with David Tod, other notable residents included the Butts family, Dr. Henry A. DuBois, Scott Vasbinder, Edward Sinchak, and Earnie Shavers. The Tod Home, along with the Butts Mansion (located on West Broad Street), the DuBois Mansion (located between North Canal Street and North Center Street), and the Neidhart Mansion (located on South Canal Street), were some of the greatest architectural designs in Newton Falls. Although none of these homes still stand, photographs and drawings by Edward Sinchak exist that are cherished bits of history. A great legend about the DuBois Mansion exists concerning Dr. Henry DuBois, who built the mansion. The legend of "the Haunted DuBois Mansion" is still believed today. In addition to glamorous mansions, Newton Falls also had several notable events. On May 24, 1970, Newton Falls hosted the Piper Rock Festival on the Louis Lightner farm. The festival was similar to Woodstock. It is estimated that more than 10,000 people attended this one-day festival, which was originally scheduled to be held in Akron, Ohio, but was shut down due to the number of tickets sold. Many nationally acclaimed acts performed at this event. Another major event in Newton Falls took place on October 25, 1972, Earnie Shavers Day, a significant occasion that took place here. Renowned boxer Earnie Shavers took part in the festivities by visiting numerous businesses in the area.

The Tod Home, located at 20 West Liberty Street, was the home of David Tod and his family. The house stood until 1973, when it was demolished. David Tod was the 25th governor of Ohio from 1861 to 1864, during the Civil War. Tod was first a Democrat but later turned Republican. He also served under Presidents James K. Polk and Millard Fillmore as an ambassador to Brazil. Although Tod was born and died in Youngstown, he had many ties to Trumbull, Geauga, and Mahoning Counties.

The Butts Mansion, often referred to as the Butts-Porter Mansion, stood at 200 Charlestown Road until 1975. Originally built between 1832 and 1834 by Dr. Henry DuBois, the home was not well-liked by Henry's father, Cornelius, upon seeing it. This led Henry to build the DuBois Mansion, which was constructed between 1838 and 1842. After the Butts Mansion was complete, it was sold by the DuBois family to Horace Stevens. Stevens then sold it to J.F. Porter. Alice Butts, granddaughter of J.F. Porter, lived in the Butts Mansion until her death in 1966. After Alice died, the house was left to her nephew Norman Root. Root died one year later, and the house was left to his widow, Eva, and two sons, Robert and Lewis. Within nine years, the Butts Mansion was in such disrepair that it was demolished. This photograph was taken in April 1975, before it was razed.

This drawing of the Butts Mansion was done by Art F. Scrimshaw. For many years, this house was referred to as the oldest home in Newton Falls. The residents of Newton Falls had such fondness for this home because of its rich history and beauty that it inspired artists like Art F. Scrimshaw and Edward Sinchak to draw the house and for it to be preserved for generations to come.

Scott McClelland Vasbinder, a police officer in Newton Falls, is photographed here while on duty. Vasbinder was born in Jefferson, Pennsylvania, on March 20, 1890. He was married to Dorothy Belle Nims and had four children. On July 5, 1932, while investigating a robbery by three men, Vasbinder was shot twice in the abdomen and died shortly after at the age of 42. The three suspects escaped but were eventually caught and executed at the Columbus Penitentiary on April 29, 1933. The alleyway next to the present-day municipal building is named Vasbinder Way, in memory of the fallen officer.

The Everett House stood on the corner of North Canal Street and East Broad Street. This photograph was taken between 1880 and 1910. Before it was owned by the Everett family, it belonged to the Reed family and was known as the Reed House. The Everett House was also used as an inn for many years. After it was demolished, many pieces of lumber were salvaged. The lumber was used in building the Neidhart home, which stood on the southwest corner of North Canal and West Broad Streets.

Edward P. Sinchak will be remembered as one of the finest art teachers of all time at Newton Falls High School. Although he has passed away, he lives on through his tiger paintings in the current high school building. Sinchak grew up in Youngstown, Ohio, and graduated from Austintown Fitch High School in 1958. Sinchak began teaching at Newton Falls High School in the early 1960s, until his retirement in the 1990s. Sinchak became a resident of Newton Falls after he began his teaching career. He built his home on McMullen Allen Road in the 1970s and hosted many glamorous parties while he lived there.

Edward Sinchak drew countless pictures of sites around Newton Falls. This drawing was of the Neidhart Mansion, which was located next to the Union Savings & Trust on the southwest corner of West Broad and North Canal Streets. The house was demolished in 1971 to make more room for the bank.

Edward Sinchak drew the home of David Tod and his family. The picture captures many details of the Tod Home. The Tod Home was located on the south side of Liberty Avenue, near North Canal Street, but was demolished in the 1970s.

Edward Sinchak is photographed with several students who have signs supporting the Newton Township police levies.

The double-covered bridge on the West Branch of the Mahoning River was drawn by Edward Sinchak. His works live on through the community, even in places that no longer stand.

The DuBois Mansion was built between 1838 and 1842 by Dr. Henry A. DuBois. The piece of land on which the house was built was owned by his father, Cornelius DuBois. Dr. Henry DuBois also built the Butts Mansion for his father, but upon Cornelius's inspection of the home, he was unhappy and asked his son to build another one. The location of the mansion was on a piece of land spinning between North Center Street, East Franklin Street, and Division Street, near the East Branch of the Mahoning River; the Lake Erie, Alliance & Wheeling Railroad rail line; and the Baltimore & Ohio rail line. Many residents of Newton Falls in the 19th and 20th centuries told stories of the DuBois home and property. These stories told tall tales of the mansion being haunted, but it was never proven. Soon, those stories turned into legends. Dr. DuBois was deemed a mad scientist and was accused of luring unsuspecting victims into his home to perform experiments on them. The DuBois Mansion burned in 1904, three years before the paper mill burned down.

A notable boxer, Earnie Shavers graduated from Newton Falls High School in 1963. Shavers boxed professionally from 1969 to 1995. Earnie Shavers Day was held in Newton Falls on October 25, 1972. Shavers, a proud Newton Falls graduate, returned to visit local businesses. He is pictured here at left during Earnie Shavers Day, boxing against Leroy Caldwell in the Newton Falls High School gymnasium.

Earnie Shavers autographed this photograph of himself. In this image, Shavers's shorts have his initials sewn into them. Shavers earned the reputation of having one of the hardest punches during his boxing matches. On September 29, 1977, Shavers boxed against Muhammad Ali in Madison Square Garden, New York. Although he lost the match, Shavers continued his successful career through the 1990s.

Here, Paul Elliott (left) of Phillip's Heating Co. meets Earnie Shavers (right). Elliott posed in his best boxing stance, while Shavers reciprocated the fists. Phillip's Heating Co. first opened in Newton Falls in 1934 and currently resides on North Canal Street.

Earnie Shavers visited Rood's Wallpaper & Paint to meet the Rood family. Photographed with Shavers is Norma Rood, the matriarch of the Rood family and owner of the business. Norma Rood shook the acclaimed boxer's hand proudly. Rood's Wallpaper & Paint was established in 1947 on Bridge Street. The business is owned and is currently operated by a third-generation family member, Karen Smith.

Earnie Shavers is all smiles at Carlo's Nightclub & Restaurant. Photographed with Shavers (center) are co-owners of Carlo's, Kenny Ferrence (left) and Bill Hyden (right).

CARLO'S NIGHTCLUB &RESTAURANT

KENNY FERRENCE, BILL HYDEN

ED'S BARBER SHOP

DEAN CHANCE, JEAN KACZYSKI, ED NUTTER

Ed's Barber Shop has been family-owned and operated in Newton Falls for more than 50 years. Photographed with Shavers (right) are, from left to right, Dean Chance; Jean Kaczyski; and Ed Nutter, the owner of Ed's Barber Shop.

109

Earnie Shavers (right) got to tour Trumbull Pattern Works to see the type of work that was done there. Photographed with Shavers is Clayton Reakes II (left), showing off some equipment inside the factory.

TRUMBULL PATTERN WORKS

CLAYTON REAKES

Earnie Shavers (left) was a longtime friend of Jim Altiere (right). Altiere, the manager of Newton Falls Auto Parts, visited and is pictured with Shavers, pointing to different tools on the wall.

NEWTON FALLS AUTO PARTS

JIM ALTIERE

Known as a "lark in the mud," the Piper Rock Festival drew over 10,000 people to a small farm on old Route 534 (now known as East River Road). This image shows one woman wading in the water and another getting ready to do the same. The festival, which was a muddy mess due to the rain, can be seen going on in the background of this image. A smaller-scale Woodstock, this event kept going despite the rain.

Bands such as the Rascals, Canned Heat, Kenny Rogers and the First Edition, Glass Harp, Smith, Marblecake, Cold Blood, Pig Iron Blues Band, Alice Cooper, Purple Image, Barnstorm (credited as Barnyard), and many more were scheduled to perform at the Piper Rock Festival. The Byrds declined to play due to the rain, in fear they would get electrocuted. However, many of these nationally acclaimed bands still performed, while some onlookers swam in the Mahoning River. Despite the huge success of this concert, the police came to shut it down during the last band's set. However, the band Pig Iron, with Canned Heat, Blind Owl, and the Rascals, continued playing for two more hours to extend the festival as long as they could.

# Nine

# BICENTENNIAL CELEBRATIONS OF 1975 AND 1976 AND THE 1985 F5 TORNADO

Newton Falls began celebrating the 200th anniversary of the signing of the Declaration of Independence in 1975. From July 5 to July 6, 1975, Newton Falls hosted a Summer Festival, which served as a predecessor to the bicentennial celebration that would occur the following year. This weekend-long forerunner festival included parades, fashion shows with period clothing, and music. Even the Ravenna Arsenal took part in 1975 by hosting a military ball and a reenactment of the Battle of Spotsylvania, Virginia. The birth of the United States was also celebrated by Newton Falls government officials, such as the mayor, and many proud residents of Newton Falls. In addition to celebrating the 200th anniversary of the nation, the 170th anniversary of Newton Falls was also celebrated. In 1976, Newton Falls celebrated the official 200th anniversary of the nation yet again, with the main attractions being the annual Fourth of July parade and fireworks.

Celebrations held a great deal of significance for the locals, especially in the tiny town of Newton Falls. In times of celebration and even in the face of tragedy, residents of the small town continually stood by one another and that would hold true in 1985. On May 31, 1985, Newton Falls suffered immense damage when an F5 tornado passed through. In addition, Niles also suffered immeasurable damage as well as cities in western Pennsylvania. While Newton Falls did not have any casualties, Niles lost nine people. Clayton Reakes II was hailed as a hero for his bravery while keeping watch over the storm from the top of the municipal building, and because of this, the sirens in Newton Falls were set off early enough for everyone to take shelter. A total of 21 tornadoes were reported in northeast Ohio and western Pennsylvania that day. The F5 tornado even touched down briefly in the Ravenna Arsenal. For safety and protection, the National Guard was called into Newton Falls after the tornado. Part of the town was completely demolished while other parts remained untouched. In 2023, a stone marker was placed on the corner of East Broad Street and South Center Street, commemorating the F5 tornado.

Each year, Newton Falls hosts a Fourth of July parade and fireworks. This image from July 4, 1976, celebrated not only the nation's independence, but the 170th anniversary of Newton Falls. The parade did not disappoint, especially with the procession of historic automobiles seen in this photograph. Onlookers watch the cars go by, with appreciation for the past.

The Warren Junior Military Band took part in the Independence Day festivities in Newton Falls on July 4, 1976. The band marched east on West Broad Street. The band was small but mighty and patriotically marched and played in celebration of the United States.

Dressing in clothing from the 1776 era was the highlight for Darlene Vasbinder. She is pictured here in a gown and bonnet representing the late 18th century. The *Newton Falls Herald* deemed this look as "Nostalgic Fashion." Vasbinder was director of the historic fashion show that was on display at the bicentennial celebration in 1975.

Many citizens of Newton Falls participated in some capacity in the bicentennial celebration. Pictured are, from left to right, Mayor Joseph Layshock, Byron Wassint, Barb Dedon, and Doris Pheiffer.

A train engine is seen in the bicentennial parade. The train represented the growth of industry accomplished as a nation in its short 200 years. The picture was taken on the corner of East Broad and North Center Streets, with the First Christian Church in the background and crowds of people watching the engine in awe.

Don Heath (left) and Howard Smith (right) show off military clothing and guns of the late 18th century. The bicentennial celebration not only celebrated America's independence, but also the birth of the United States as a nation 200 years ago.

From left to right, William Hawkins, Mayor Joseph Layshock, and Theo Montgomery are pictured with the bicentennial flag. William Hawkins was part of the Trumbull County Bicentennial Commission, and Theo Montgomery was a trustee for Newton Township. These three government men proudly hold the flag to celebrate the nation's independence.

# SIXTH

# NATIONAL ENCAMPMENT

# SVR

JUNE 20, 21, 22, 1975

RAVENNA U.S. ARMY

AMMUNITION PLANT

RAVENNA

OHIO

Battle Re-enactment
May 12, 1864 * Spotsylvania, Va.
on
SUNDAY June 22, 1975 * 2:00PM.

HISTORY RELIVED
CIVIL WAR * INFANTRY
ARTILLERY * CAVALRY

BATTLE DRILL COMPETITION
PARADE
MILITARY BALL

Celebrating the 200th Anniversary of the
United States Army
as part of
this Nation's Bicentennial

Printed As A
Training Mission By
350th PSYOP

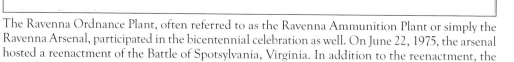

The Ravenna Ordnance Plant, often referred to as the Ravenna Ammunition Plant or simply the Ravenna Arsenal, participated in the bicentennial celebration as well. On June 22, 1975, the arsenal hosted a reenactment of the Battle of Spotsylvania, Virginia. In addition to the reenactment, the arsenal also hosted a military ball, a parade, and a drill competition.

A group of festival participants dressed in 18th-century clothing posed in front of a sign with a list of festivities, including a band concert, fashion-style show, flag raising, and an art show. This photograph was taken on July 6, 1975. Celebrations of the bicentennial began as early as June in the Newton Falls area.

On May 31, 1985, an F5 tornado destroyed many parts of Newton Falls. An F5 tornado is nicknamed the "Finger of God," and the nickname fits well after seeing scenes of destruction in this photograph. A house and part of the high school were severely damaged by the 1985 F5 tornado that came through Newton Falls on May 31. Although many houses and buildings were destroyed, quite a few survived the triple-digit winds.

Scenes from the Standard Oil (So-Ohio) gas station show damage to the building on the corner of North Canal Street and West Broad Street. Debris is piled up in the background, while cars and trucks try to make their way through the rubble. The building was destroyed by the tornado.

An aerial view after the tornado shows a house completely ripped from its foundation, while other houses only suffered minor damage. The aerial view also shows damaged trees. Onlookers look on in horror at the site of the uprooted house.

National Guardsmen are seen in this photograph on the West Broad Street Bridge. The guards were originally sent to Newton Falls to protect the citizens from any looting. The Union Savings & Trust building, called Bank One in 1985, is seen untouched, while the Circle Bar, just several feet away, had its roof torn off.

First Row Video, Plants & Such, Davis Insurance, Bailey Furniture Company, and Kistler's all suffered damage to their buildings on West Broad Street. Debris from the tornado is still present on the road. Several men direct traffic to help out the city in need. Several windows were torn out by the heavy winds of the tornado above these businesses. Many of these buildings still stand today, despite the high amount of damage they endured.

The junior high school and gymnasium buildings were greatly damaged in the tornado, but the high school and library stood strong. Pictured here is the gymnasium and the massive damage it suffered. Bricks and rubble are piled high in this photograph, and the walls were ripped from the side. The school speed limit sign is still present and did not incur any damage.

An aerial view shows many areas completely leveled and others unscathed. This view shows North Canal, South Canal, and West Broad Streets. The Ford dealership is present but leveled, while the municipal building and the house to the left are still in one piece. The devastation and loss that was left by the tornado were greatly felt among the residents of Newton Falls.

A local resident on a tractor was guided to proceed straight by a National Guardsman. Many cleanup crews are seen in this photograph, trying to restore the city to what it once was. Power lines were in need of restoration after the wind damage. Another Guardsman directs traffic on the opposite side of the street.

The aerial view shows Charlestown Road, West Broad Street, and Canal Street. The high school building is seen, with major damage to the gymnasium. First Christian Church is present as well as the parsonage. Bank One and the water tower are seen in the center of this image as well as the downtown area on West Broad Street. The post office and the American Legion Hall, also present, were severely damaged. A new structure for the American Legion was erected on East River Road, and the post office was housed in the skating rink building on Ridge Road.

Piles and piles of rubble are photographed here. The piles of rubble in Newton Falls and surrounding cities incurred on May 31, 1985, may have been cleaned up, but it never was the same city again. Although the devastation leveled many buildings, the city of Newton Falls and its residents came together to clean up the damage and made the city stronger than ever.

# Storm watch pays off in Newton Falls

By ANDY GRAY
Tribune Staff Writer

NEWTON FALLS — Whenever a bad storm is approaching the city, Clayton Reakes usually can be found on top of the city building, waiting to sound the emergency sirens if it becomes dangerous.

Most of the time, Reakes' trips to the roof turn out to be nothing, and the only result is that he leaves a lot wetter than he arrived.

But Friday, Reakes' presence on the roof may be the main reason why there were no fatalities from the tornado that ripped through the center of town.

Maj. Calvin Taylor of the Ohio National Guard said in an Associated Press story that the sirens went off early enough for about 150 people at the American Legion Hall next door to take cover before the tornado hit. The hall was demolished Wednesday because of the tornado damage.

For Reakes and Larry Sembach, who was on the roof until minutes before the tornado struck, it was justification for their efforts after years of discouragement.

"I felt good because we said we needed it (the storm watch) for a long time," Reakes said.

Reakes is captain and Sembach is lieutenant of the city's safety police reserve. Both have received schooling in storm watching, and police are instructed to contact either of them when a weather warning comes over its computer.

"We did it (set off the sirens) once before," Reakes said. "A (former) councilman told us we shouldn't be up there, that we were scaring the

Tribune/Andy

Clayton Reakes was on the roof of the Newton Falls city building before the tornado struck Frid and he was able to have the city's emergency sirens set off before the twister hit. A colonel v the Ohio National Guard said that warning probably saved the lives of many city residents.

people for nothing. I wonder what he'd say now."

Reakes said he and the other reserves have continued to do the storm watch because it can "save lives. If we can get a warning out, they can save lives."

Reakes has spent most of the time since the tornado trying to clean the site of his business, Trumbull Pattern Works. The top level of the building was destroyed by the twister.

While working, several people have come up and told him that the sirens saved their lives.

"A guy who lives down the street came up to me today (Wednesday) and said if it wasn't for the siren, his wife and kids would have been killed," Reakes said.

The man was able to get his family into the basement because he heard the siren. The tornado leveled his home.

Before Friday, Reakes' trips to the roof of city hall were routine, so routine that even his wife, Sarah,

wasn't worried when he left house.

"It's so routine for him to there watching for a tornado, when it hit, I thought it was a (alarm)," she said. "I never us think about it when he went ou a tornado watch. I will now."

Reakes carries a pager with at all times and has a mobile p in his car so the police can co him when a tornado watch is ca Reakes and Sembach also j

See WATCHERS, Pag

Clayton Reakes II was the city of Newton Falls's storm watcher. Reakes often went to the roof of the municipal building, and if an alert was needed, the sirens would be set off. On Friday, May 31, 1985, Reakes climbed to the top of the municipal building, not expecting anything to be wrong. But after some alarming weather, the siren sounded. Reakes was the hero in Newton Falls to so many residents, who took safety after hearing the looming tornado siren throughout the city. Reakes owned Trumbull Pattern Works, and thankfully, only the roof was damaged during the F5 tornado. Reakes died two years later and was buried in the west-side cemetery in Newton Falls. On his gravestone is a picture of a tornado, along with the finger of God.

After the tornado hit Newton Falls, Dan Ross of the State Soil & Conservation Department and Mike Blau, the Newton Falls city manager, met to form a plan to clean up the West Branch of the Mahoning River. This photograph was taken on June 19, 1985, with both gentlemen holding a map that says, "Drainage Debris from tornadoes, 5/31/1985."

# DISCOVER THOUSANDS OF LOCAL HISTORY BOOKS FEATURING MILLIONS OF VINTAGE IMAGES

Arcadia Publishing, the leading local history publisher in the United States, is committed to making history accessible and meaningful through publishing books that celebrate and preserve the heritage of America's people and places.

## Find more books like this at
## www.arcadiapublishing.com

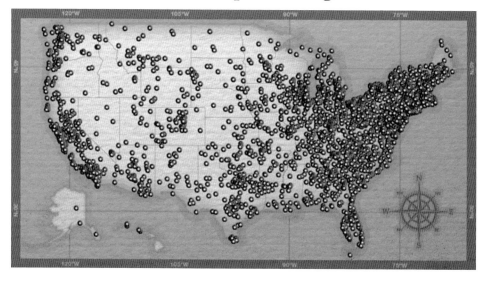

Search for your hometown history, your old stomping grounds, and even your favorite sports team.

Consistent with our mission to preserve history on a local level, this book was printed in South Carolina on American-made paper and manufactured entirely in the United States. Products carrying the accredited Forest Stewardship Council (FSC) label are printed on 100 percent FSC-certified paper.

MADE IN THE USA